Good Morning
GOD

LISA STERLING

Brilliant Books Literary
137 Forest Park Lane Thomasville
North Carolina 27360 USA

Because of the dynamic nature of the Internet, any web addresses or links contained in this book may have changed since publication and may no longer be valid. The views expressed in this work are solely those of the author and do not necessarily reflect the views of the publisher, and the publisher hereby disclaims any responsibility for them.

ISBN: 979-8-88945-039-9
eISBN: 979-8-88945-040-5

Printed in the United States of America

DEDICATION

In loving memory of my husband.

To my readers:

Thank you for taking the time to purchase my book. I really appreciate it. If you find as you go through the book and see some blank pages you can use that to write down your own thoughts or anything else that may come to mind. Enjoy the book.